THE GET

Ready!

Monthly Personal
Finance Guidebook

TONY STEUER, CLU, LA, CPFFE

LIFE
INSURANCE
SAGE
PRESS

Published by Life Insurance Sage Press
Alameda, CA
tonysteuer.com

Distributed by River Grove Books

Design and composition by Greenleaf Book Group
Cover design by Greenleaf Book Group
Cover icon from flaticon.com. Medical History by Linector.
Get Ready! Financial Calendar images by Maggie Stilwell (maggiestilwell.com).

Publisher's Cataloging-in-Publication data is available.

Print ISBN: 978-1-7342100-1-9

First Edition

Introduction

WELCOME TO *THE GET READY!* *Monthly Personal Finance Guidebook,* a month-by-month fill-in guide that offers you checklists and notes pages critical to capturing the information you need most for your financial first aid kit. Just like you would want to make sure your medical first aid kit is stocked with everything you need, this guidebook is a key item in your financial first aid kit to guarantee that you're financially ready for any situation or event.

Providing you with a year of guided financial direction, these pages will help you prepare for any financial emergency, organize your finances for your family members (in the event that you fall ill), have your documents ready when you're applying for a loan or filing taxes, and easily monitor your financial life. This is a monthly management guide that will show you how to get everything in order, so you can take good financial care of yourself and the people most important to you.

The guidebook serves as a financial companion to *Get Ready!: A Step-by-Step Planner for Maintaining Your Financial First Aid Kit.* It can also be used on a stand-alone basis. Either way, you can start during any month of the year and follow its prompts and instructions to receive coaching throughout your entire financial year. The next year, you then have the option of getting a new guidebook to continue to keep your financial life on track.

HOW TO USE THIS MONTHLY PERSONAL FINANCE GUIDEBOOK

Each monthly spread focuses on a specific goal or action item, with a checklist on the left to help you accomplish that month's goal and a financial SOAP note on the right for you to fill in with your personal finance information.

Monthly Checklist

The checklist guides you through each month's topic and provides you with relevant details and information for reaching your goal. You can find downloadable PDFs of all the Get Ready! worksheets referenced in this guide by going to tonysteuer.com and accessing the Get Ready! Toolkit.

SOAP Note

First responders in medical emergencies use something called a SOAP note as a way for them to effectively and efficiently evaluate a situation. The SOAP note is a form of documentation that allows them to capture the information most needed and put it in an easy-to-read format. It includes four areas:

S: Subjective (what the medical issue or situation is)
O: Objective (facts or data, such as vital signs)
A: Assessment (the diagnosis)
P: Plan (how to proceed)

In *The Get Ready! Monthly Personal Finance Guidebook,* the SOAP notes pages will help you capture, record, and assess the financial information you need most so that within a year, you can be as prepared as possible in all the major facets of your financial life. The SOAP note is designed to be clear and concise to keep you focused and provide you with an organized approach to completing the monthly task. You'll be prompted to fill in key information and then will be guided toward identifying steps around an achievable timeline and monitoring your progress. Following this standard format can enable you to easily communicate your finances to others, including family members, financial advisors, financial planners, or insurance agents. Each month's SOAP note may be completed by you, someone in your family or tribe, or whoever you may choose to designate.

If you're leading or facilitating a group, you can download a checklist to start your own Get Ready! Financial Preparedness Club with monthly group discussion questions.

GET READY!

The Get Ready! Monthly Personal Finance Guidebook, a key part of your financial first aid kit, is built on Get Ready! principles and will help ensure you're as financially prepared as possible for life situations or events. It can literally be a financial lifesaver. GET READY! stands for:

Goals:	Be prepared. It's important to have financial goals so that you can be in charge of your financial future.
Educate yourself:	Become financially literate. Take the time to understand your financial life. Never make a financial decision that you don't understand. Instead, keep it simple.
Track:	Be alert. It's important to keep an eye on all areas of your financial life, so you can achieve your goals.
Review:	Know your options. After determining that a financial product will fit your goals, determine which product configuration is right for you. Make sure to evaluate all of your options. If you need help, seek a qualified advisor.
Expenses:	Do you know what you're paying for? Watch your expenses/costs: It's common to only think about the primary cost of an asset or an investment along with the expected return. However, there are often hidden costs and/or high expenses that increase the amount of money you pay for something and/or the return on your investment. You may not be able to make significant adjustments to your income; however, you can make adjustments to your costs.
Assemble information:	Most of us have our financial life scattered in many places. Take the time to bring it all together by creating a financial first aid kit.
Details:	Take the time to review the details of financial products and services. As John Wooden said, "It's the little details that are vital. Little things make big things happen." Make smart and realistic financial decisions. A good rule of thumb is, if it sounds too good to be true, then it probably is.
Yearly review:	Life is full of changes. It's important to monitor all aspects of your financial life to see if changes should be made and if you are maximizing value. Having a financial calendar will help you stay on track. Part of this includes doing a financial background check (credit reports and so on) to make sure your financial history is correct.

Thank you for taking this important step toward financial preparedness. It's my mission to help you Get Ready! for life changing events by showing you how to put together and maintain a financial first aid kit, so you can be prepared for any financial emergency.

Note: Please be advised that I am not an accountant, investment advisor, or attorney, and the content in this guidebook should not be considered as tax, investing, or legal advice.

Tony

The Get Ready! Financial Calendar

The Get Ready! financial calendar offers you an at-a-glance overview of your entire financial year. Each month focuses on a goal or action item to help put you in charge of all the major aspects of your financial life. You can use this calendar with your financial first aid kit to look ahead, plan for, and organize your important financial information.

GET
Ready!
FINANCIAL CALENDAR

JANUARY
Organize your financial documents

FEBRUARY
Monitor your financial dashboard (cash flow and net worth statement)

MARCH
Review your loans and expenses

APRIL
File federal and state income tax returns
Check your income tax withholding

MAY
Review your financial emergency plan

JUNE
Hold a family financial meeting
Review and communicate goals and priorities

JULY
Review beneficiaries and estate planning documents to make sure they are current

AUGUST
Review your personal investment policy statement (investments and allocations)

SEPTEMBER
Review insurance policies

OCTOBER
Open enrollment for group employee benefits and Individual Health Insurance, and Medicare begins

NOVEMBER
Order credit reports and consumer reports

DECEMBER
Wrap up loose ends
Look for unclaimed property

Organize Your Financial Documents

 Goal: Take this month to assemble and organize your financial documents from the prior year.

Being financially organized will help you prepare for any financial emergency, whether it's a natural disaster, disability, or death. It's important to be financially prepared at all stages of your life, whether you are just starting out, in the middle of your working life, or in retirement.

☐ **Gather Together Your Financial Documents from the Prior Year.** If you have financial documents from previous years, you can create separate piles for them, but set them aside for now. The goal for this month is only to organize your records from the preceding year.

☐ **Organize Your Records by Type.** Inevitably, you'll encounter all kinds of documents and receipts. I recommend organizing them into these major types:

☐ Personal papers and documents

☐ Income

☐ Assets

☐ Home and real estate/real property

☐ Debts, personal loans, living expenses, and taxes

☐ Insurance

☐ Retirement plans

☐ Estate planning

☐ Identity monitoring (credit reports and consumer reports)

I recommend storing your financial documents in a designated binder, specifically organized so that you can have everything you need at your fingertips, no matter the financial situation. To help you know what to assemble and how to put together your binder, a crucial part of your personal financial first aid kit, *Get Ready!: A Step-by-Step Planner for Maintaining Your Financial First Aid Kit* walks you through the steps for doing this. Once you gather these financial records, I also encourage you to back them up and keep them secure in one or more of the following places: 1) a fire-proof safe, 2) a safe-deposit box, 3) your cloud storage account, like Apple iCloud or Dropbox, for digital storage, and/or 4) a USB thumb drive for digital storage, which you can then keep safe in your personal financial binder.

☐ **Update Your Records.** Your financial life is one that is dynamic and always changing. Once you've assembled and organized your documents this month, you'll want to keep them up-to-date. Here are some best practices for doing this:

☐ Add current statements or documents to the records you've already assembled.

☐ Organize them into your existing system, so you won't need to spend time reorganizing and integrating them at a later point.

☐ You can update your records once per year (always during the month of February, for example) or throughout the year.

☐ Store the documents only for the recommended number of years. You can access a fillable Personal Papers and Legal Documents worksheet at tonysteuer.com. It offers timing guidelines for key financial documents.

☐ Shred or destroy documents that are no longer needed, but take note of items (described in the Personal Papers and Legal Documents worksheet in the Get Ready! planner that should be kept indefinitely).

Organize Your Financial Documents

SUBJECTIVE

Summarize the goal for January. How do you feel about it?

_____

_____

_____

OBJECTIVE

Fill in the following table as you gather and update your financial documents:

	LAST UPDATED/ REVIEWED:	MONTH TO REVIEW
Personal Papers and Documents		
Income		
Assets		
Home and Real Estate/Real Property		
Debts and Expenses		
Insurance		
Retirement Plans		
Estate Planning		
Identity Monitoring		

Where will you store these records? _____

Who will you communicate this to, so they may access the records if needed? _____

How often do you plan to update these documents? _____

ASSESSMENT

Based on your findings above, how are you doing financially at this point in time? Be specific.

_____

_____

_____

_____

_____

_____

_____

PLAN

What do you plan to do to improve your financial situation this year? Describe actions you will take and provide a timeline for completion with checkpoints and a deadline.

_____

_____

_____

_____

_____

_____

_____

Monitor Your Financial Dashboard

 Goal: Review your Cash Flow and Personal Balance Sheet. This lets you see how you did last year and if you want to make any changes for the new year.

☐ **Look at Your Cash Flow Statement—Your Budget.** Understanding your cash flow, or budget, will help you get financially organized so that you can be ready to make informed financial decisions for the coming year. You can access a fillable Cash Flow Statement worksheet at tonysteuer.com.

   ☐ **Review how much money you have coming in (your income) and how much you are spending (your expenses).** Your expenses should always be lower than your income. If they're higher, you know that you must find a way to either increase your income or reduce your expenses. If you have excess funds, they can be used for savings.

   ☐ **Here at the beginning of the year, is your cash flow positive or negative?** What, if anything, do you need to do about it?

☐ **Look at Your Net Worth Statement.** Reviewing your Net Worth Statement will allow you to see whether or not you are financially solvent. Your net worth is the total value of everything you own (your assets), less what you owe (your liabilities). Is your net worth increasing? If not, you can make adjustments to your cash flow now, so that you can get on track. You can access a fillable Net Worth Statement worksheet at tonysteuer.com.

☐ **Look at Your Financial Ratios.** Financial ratios are general guidelines to help you see if your financial life is on a healthy, organized track. Everyone's situation is different, so if your ratios aren't in line with the recommended ratios, this is a sign that you should make adjustments that will allow you to meet your personal needs and goals. You can access a fillable Financial Ratios Statement worksheet at tonysteuer.com that will help you calculate your financial ratios and assess where you currently are with your financial life. I recommend using these ratios to mark your progress:

   ☐ **Emergency Fund.** Make sure you have sufficient cash on hand to be able to cover expenses in the event of a loss of income for 3–6 months.

   ☐ **Liquidity Ratio.** This is how much of your assets are in cash or cash equivalents. Your liquidity ratio should be at least 15%.

   ☐ **Debt-to-Income Ratio.** Lenders use this ratio to determine the acceptable amount of debt. Your goal should be to keep this below 36%.

   ☐ **Savings Ratio.** This ratio has a wide range of 12–20% and depends on your current age, your desired retirement age, and the amount of money you've already saved.

   ☐ **Net Worth Ratio.** It's important to determine if your net worth is on track. Your goal should be to have this ratio equal your net worth.

Monitor Your Financial Dashboard

SUBJECTIVE

Summarize the goal for February. How do you feel about it?

_____

_____

_____

OBJECTIVE

Record your observations or findings in the table below:

CASH FLOW	NET WORTH	FINANCIAL RATIOS
Total Income: $_____	Assets: $_____	Emergency Fund: _____ months. To calculate this, divide your fixed monthly expenses by your liquid assets.
Total Expenses: $_____	Liabilities: $_____	Liquidity Ratio: _____%. To calculate this, divide your total net worth by your liquid assets.
Gain/Loss: $_____	Net Worth (assets minus liabilities): $_____	Debt to Income Ratio: _____%. To calculate this, divide your total housing costs plus any of your other debt payments by your gross income.
		Savings Ratio: $_____. This is the amount you save each month divided by your gross income.
		Net Worth Ratio: $_____. To find this number, multiply your annual gross income by your age, then divide by 10.

ASSESSMENT

Based on your findings above, how are you doing financially at this point in time? Be specific.

_____

_____

_____

_____

_____

_____

_____

_____

PLAN

What do you plan to do to improve your financial situation this year? Describe actions you will take and provide a timeline for completion with checkpoints and a deadline.

_____

_____

_____

_____

_____

_____

_____

Review Your Loans and Expenses

 Goal: Review your loans and expenses to reduce your outlay.

☐ **Review Your Debt Repayment Strategy.**

　☐ **Make a list of all your existing debts, including mortgages, car loans, credit card balances, and student loans.** As you do this, record the loan balance, minimum payment, and interest rate. You can access a fillable Debt worksheet at tonysteuer.com.

　☐ **Rank each debt by interest rate.** I recommend paying off your highest-cost debt as quickly as possible and then working your way down to pay off your lowest-cost debt. When you make a payment on a credit card or loan, always pay more than the minimum balance due; if you only pay the minimum balance, it could take you years to pay it off.

　☐ **Watch your debt and avoid consolidation.** A debt consolidation loan is a refinanced loan with an extended repayment period, which means it will take longer to pay off your debt. Consolidation loans do not reduce your overall debt or outstanding payments. In particular:

　　☐ **Mortgages.** Review the terms of your home mortgage periodically, as you may be able to reduce your interest rate or have it guaranteed for a longer period. There are two main types of mortgages: fixed rate and adjustable rate. A fixed rate mortgage has a guaranteed interest rate and payments for a set period of time, usually 15 or 30 years. An adjustable rate mortgage (ARM) will have a fixed rate for an initial period, after which time the interest rate can be increased or decreased. But note that refinancing charges can be high, so be sure to include these in your calculation.

　　☐ **Credit cards.** Credit cards have high interest rates and are the most expensive debt. Ask for a better rate for your current card(s), or seek alternatives; if you do move your debt to a different card, be wary of balance transfer fees. I also recommend making it a practice to redeem your credit card rewards, as sometimes these expire. Know that cash rewards can usually be redeemed monthly, so if you haven't been doing this, now is a good time.

　　☐ **College loans.** Be wary of college debt consolidation loans. If you move from a US government loan to a private loan, you will lose the option to use income-based repayment plans, like Pay As You Earn (PAYE) or Income-Based Repayment (IBR).

☐ **Reduce Your Expenses.** After you review your debt portfolio, consider the following tips for continuing to bring down your expenses in the future. You can access fillable Expenses worksheets at tonysteuer.com.

　☐ **Pay all bills upon receipt.** This will save you from incurring late fees if a bill becomes buried.

　☐ **Set up reminders for bills that you are expecting.** Sometimes, bills get lost in the mail or lost in spam filters. If you create reminders, you'll not only know bills that are coming but also have an easier time of anticipating and preparing for that cost.

　☐ **Review your expenses periodically to see if there are any you can eliminate.** Services that you either no longer use or use infrequently, such as gym memberships or subscriptions, may be able to be removed from your list of expenses.

　☐ **Contact your service providers to request better pricing packages.** Many companies, especially phone and cable companies, introduce new pricing packages from time to time and allow you to make adjustments to your plan. This can be one way to cut costs.

MARCH SOAP NOTE

Review Your Loans and Expenses

SUBJECTIVE

Summarize the goal for March. How do you feel about it?

_____

_____

_____

OBJECTIVE

Fill in the following table as you think through your debt repayment strategy:

LOAN/DEBT NAME	LOAN BALANCE	MINIMUM PAYMENT	INTEREST RATE	PRIORITY/ RANK	CREDIT CARD REWARDS REDEEMED?

ASSESSMENT

Based on your findings above, how are you doing financially at this point in time? Be specific.

_____

_____

_____

_____

_____

_____

_____

_____

_____

PLAN

What do you plan to do to improve your financial situation this year? Describe actions you will take and provide a timeline for completion with checkpoints and a deadline.

_____

_____

_____

_____

_____

_____

_____

_____

Review Your Tax Planning

 Goal: Monitor Your Tax Strategy.

Tax planning is for everyone, not just the wealthy. By reviewing and planning your tax strategy, you can minimize your taxes. Here are some steps that you should take every year to help you make sure that you are minimizing your taxable outlay:

☐ **File Your Income Tax Return.**

    ☐ **Check to see that you receive all your necessary tax documents on time.**

    ☐ **Be sure to always save and assemble your receipts, including receipts for charitable donations, so you can take all available deductions.** An accountant or tax software program, like TurboTax, can guide you on this.

    ☐ **Use the Get Ready! Tax Documents worksheet to track your expected tax documents.** You can access a fillable Tax Documents worksheet at tonysteuer.com.

    ☐ **File your taxes on time.** Tax returns are due on April 15 (if April 15 is on a weekend, the IRS and individual states usually extend the due date to the following Monday, but check the IRS and your state's tax websites to confirm).

    ☐ **Request an extension (or extensions) if necessary.** States follow different rules, so check with the tax authority in your state to avoid fines and penalties for missing deadlines.

    ☐ **Review your tax returns carefully to ensure you are maximizing all of your deductions.** This includes using tax-advantaged retirement accounts and college savings accounts.

    ☐ **Determine if you may need to pay estimated taxes as a result of under-withholding or being self-employed.** Estimated taxes are due four times a year. Each period has a specific payment deadline, typically April 15, June 15, September 15, and January 15 of the following year (unless the 15th falls on the weekend, in which case the due date is usually the following Monday). Check www.irs.gov and your state tax bureau to confirm the deadlines.

☐ **Check Your Tax Withholding.**

    ☐ **Use the IRS Withholding Estimator, a useful calculator available to you through www.irs.gov, to perform a quick paycheck checkup.** This calculator helps you identify your tax withholding to make sure you have the right amount of tax withheld from your work paycheck. Checking your withholding can help protect you against having too little tax withheld and, as a result, facing an unexpected tax bill or penalty during tax time the following year. At the same time, with the average refund topping $2,800, you may instead prefer to have less tax withheld up front in order to receive more in your paychecks.

    ☐ **File a W-4 with your employer if you determine that you need to change your tax withholding.**

    ☐ **Review your property taxes.**

    ☐ **Use an online service, like www.zillow.com, to view comparable home-price values and an estimate on your home.** If your property value has decreased, you can usually request that your property be reassessed to determine if your property tax can be reduced.

Review Your Tax Planning

SUBJECTIVE

Summarize the goal for April. How do you feel about it?

_____

_____

_____

OBJECTIVE

Fill in the following table as you make your way through the checklist this month:

List the Tax Documents You Received	
Record the Date When You Filed Your Income Taxes	
Date When You Checked Your Income Tax Withholding	
Date When You Reviewed Your Potential Deductions	
What Estimated Taxes Are Needed?	
Date When you Reviewed Your Property Tax Assessment Value	

ASSESSMENT

Based on your findings above, how are you doing financially at this point in time? Be specific.

_____

_____

_____

_____

_____

_____

_____

_____

_____

PLAN

What do you plan to do to improve your financial situation this year? Describe actions you will take and provide a timeline for completion with checkpoints and a deadline.

_____

_____

_____

_____

_____

_____

_____

_____

_____

MAY CHECKLIST

Review Your Financial Emergency Plan

 Goal: Set up your financial emergency plan by creating a critical emergency action list and a financial first aid kit.

☐ **Assemble a Financial First Aid Kit.** Get Ready! is a robust yet practical system designed to prepare you for any financial emergency, help you organize your finances, and show you how to monitor your financial life. I encourage you to continue to work on completing all the components of your financial first aid kit, so you can be ready and stay ready.

☐ **Create a Critical Emergency Action List.** During an emergency, you may have limited time to gather what you need, lose access to the internet, or realize you're lacking certain supplies. I recommend putting together a critical emergency action list to ensure you and your family know what to do in the moment.

   ☐ **Make a list of the steps you'll take.** Every family is unique, so a one-size-fits-all action plan may not address all your family's needs. It's important to take the time to think through the steps that are essential to you and your family. You can access the Critical Emergency Action worksheet from tonysteuer.com to receive guidance on steps you can take.

   ☐ **Review your emergency plan with all members of your family.**

   ☐ **Choose a meeting location for your family in the event of an emergency.** It's a good idea to set primary as well as secondary locations.

   ☐ **Review your evacuation procedures.**

   ☐ **Know how to shut off the water, gas, and main electrical switch to your home.**

   ☐ **Establish a communication plan.** Set up an out-of-area contact that you and other family members can relay information to. Determine if you and your family will also use an online resource to communicate with one another. Make sure everyone knows and understands your communication plan.

   ☐ **Make sure your fire extinguishers are accessible and know how to use them.** Keep in mind that sometimes, fire extinguishers need to be refreshed, so check these regularly.

   ☐ **Monitor your smoke, CO_2, and other alarms.** Replace the batteries in these and test each of them. A good practice is to do this twice a year when the time changes.

   ☐ **Know what items you will want to take with you in the event of an evacuation.**

☐ **Make a List of Documents You Will Need in an Emergency.** The documents that you will need in an emergency include those that can help you manage your financial life. These may include driver's licenses (or other identification), passports, medical information and medication details, and insurance policy summaries (with the company name and your policy number). Optimally, you should have either your physical Get Ready! planner and binder or a digital equivalent.

☐ **Prepare a Physical Emergency Kit.** Your emergency kit should include a first aid kit and enough supplies to last 3–5 days. Be sure to include medications, along with prescriptions. You can access a fillable Emergency Kit worksheet at tonysteuer.com.

Review Your Financial Emergency Plan

SUBJECTIVE

Summarize the goal for May. How do you feel about it?

_____

_____

_____

OBJECTIVE

Fill in the following table as you review and prepare your financial and critical emergency action plan:

ITEMS TO REVIEW:	NOTES
Your Emergency Plan	
Your Emergency Meeting Location(s)	
Your Communication Plan	
Your Evacuation Plan (Steps to Take)	
Your Financial First Aid Kit (Financial Documents)	
You Emergency Kit Location	

ASSESSMENT

Based on your findings above, how are you doing financially at this point in time? Be specific.

_____

_____

_____

_____

_____

_____

_____

_____

_____

PLAN

What do you plan to do to improve your financial situation this year? Describe actions you will take and provide a timeline for completion with checkpoints and a deadline.

_____

_____

_____

_____

_____

_____

_____

_____

_____

Hold a Family Financial Meeting

 Goal: Review and communicate your financial goals, priorities, and intentions.

In the month of June, bring together your close family members, including your spouse, domestic partner, children, and/or parents, to discuss your financial goals, priorities, and wishes to allow your family to align themselves with the financial actions you're proposing and weigh in with their thoughts and perspectives. Good communication is the key to managing your family's finances. It can also provide the entire family with a sense of unity around a concrete target.

- ☐ **Set Up Your Family Meeting.**

  - ☐ **Invite every stakeholder.** Each person in the family who works with or benefits from "house money" should be invited, including your kids. Note that involving kids in family financial planning can be a great way for them to learn and become financially literate.

  - ☐ **Schedule the family meeting like you would a business meeting.** Establish a clear agenda and purpose, so the meeting will be productive. Because discussions about finances can be emotional, a meeting plan will allow everyone to more easily stick to the script.

- ☐ **Guide the Discussion during the Meeting.**

  - ☐ **Make sure to cover all the necessary topics.** Are you focusing on maximizing retirement savings? Is your family saving for your children to go to college? Each objective that's relevant to your family's finances needs to be covered, including discreet goals for making them happen.

  - ☐ **Provide opportunities for everyone to talk.** It's important that everyone in the family has a chance to communicate what their financial priorities, goals, and objectives are. Remember that you are striving to make a plan that works for all members of the family.

  - ☐ **Work together to set short-term, intermediate-term, and long-term financial goals.**

  - ☐ **Designate financial family roles.** Based on the goals you and your family set, you can define roles or jobs for people that will help ensure the goals are accomplished and also provide everyone with a sense of ownership in the family's finances. Typically, one person handles the majority of financial tasks, such as paying bills and managing investments, but other family members can take on responsibilities as needed.

- ☐ **Create a Family Transition Plan.** Once family roles are designated, the family should devise a system and plan for how other family members would take over for them in the event of an emergency. You can access the Stepping In worksheet at tonysteuer.com for a useful resource that will help your family be prepared if someone else needs to step in to take over the finances. I recommend also doing the following:

  - ☐ **Share the family's financial information and any personal financial information with your spouse or domestic partner.** It's a good idea to coordinate your financial lives so that you can each take over for the other person if needed. Doing this can also help you reduce expenses by combining certain accounts, such as cellular service and online services.

  - ☐ **Communicate where your financial documents and any information about your wishes are located.**

  - ☐ **Complete your Get Ready! Financial First Aid Kit,** so that all the other pieces of your financial life will already be in place.

  - ☐ **Make a plan in the event of your death.** One way to take care of your family financially is to ensure they know what to do if you pass away.

Hold a Family Financial Meeting

SUBJECTIVE

Summarize the goal for June. How do you feel about it?

_____

_____

_____

OBJECTIVE

Fill in the following table based on the discussion during your family meeting:

Date of Family Financial Meeting	
Goals	
Priorities	
Roles	
Emergency Plan Created?	
Transition Plan—Who Will Step In?	

ASSESSMENT

Based on your findings above, how are you doing financially at this point in time? Be specific.

_____

_____

_____

_____

_____

_____

_____

_____

PLAN

What do you plan to do to improve your financial situation this year? Describe actions you will take and provide a timeline for completion with checkpoints and a deadline.

_____

_____

_____

_____

_____

_____

_____

_____

Review Your Beneficiaries and Estate Plan

 Goal: Review your beneficiaries and estate plan to ensure that they are current.

☐ **Review Your Beneficiary Designations.**

  ☐ **Make sure beneficiaries are designated on your applicable policies, accounts, and estate-planning documents.** To keep track of these, you can access the Get Ready! worksheets you'll need at tonysteuer.com.

  ☐ **Update beneficiary designations as needed.** This is important if there's been a major life event in your family such as a birth, death, marriage, divorce, or retirement. Know that beneficiary designations take priority over wills and trusts, so if, for example, an ex-spouse is still your named beneficiary, they will receive the proceeds.

  ☐ **Name a contingent beneficiary in the event that your primary beneficiary predeceases you.** Consider naming a nonprofit organization if you would prefer that they receive the money.

  ☐ **If needed, consult with a qualified tax advisor or attorney.** There are tax consequences that go with naming a trust as the beneficiary for your retirement plan and annuities. It's best to consult with a professional to see what this looks like.

☐ **Review Your Estate-Planning Documents.** I recommend making sure you have the following in place and with accurate and updated information. You can access all the Get Ready! worksheets you'll need for these at tonysteuer.com.

  ☐ **Power of Attorney (POA) form.** This is a legal document you complete to appoint someone else to make legal and financial decisions on your behalf in case you are no longer able to do so.

  ☐ **Health-care directives/advanced directive/Health-Care Power of Attorney form.** An advance directive allows you to specify what types of treatments you do and don't want at the end of your life. It also allows you to designate another person (usually your spouse or other family member) to communicate your specified health-care decisions in the event of your incapacitation.

  ☐ **Final arrangements document.** This document allows you to communicate your wishes for your remains and memorial services.

  ☐ **Ethical Will.** An ethical will is a personal document that you create to communicate your values, experiences, and life lessons to your family.

  ☐ **Will.** A will is a legally enforceable declaration of how you want your property or assets to be distributed after death.

  ☐ **Trust.** A trust (or trust fund) is a legal entity that allows you (the grantor, donor, or settlor) to transfer assets to another person or organization (the trustee).

  ☐ **Digital Estate Plan.** This is a plan that enables you to say what you'd like to do with your digital assets after your death. It includes your plans for your email accounts, websites, blogs, social media accounts, internet membership sites, cloud storage, and other internet- and software-related activities.

  ☐ **Pet Estate Plan.** Pets are often overlooked in estate planning, yet they are a part of the family. Make sure to write down the details about your wishes for your pets.

Communicating any other wishes you have about your general estate plan to others is also important. If people don't know your wishes, they won't be able to carry them out for you.

Review Your Beneficiaries and Estate Plan

SUBJECTIVE

Summarize the goal for July. How do you feel about it?

_____

_____

_____

OBJECTIVE

Fill in the following table as you go through the process of reviewing your estate plan:

	DATE REVIEWED
Life Insurance—Group and Individual	
Retirement Plans—401(k), 403(b), IRAs	
Brokerage Account(s)	
Bank Account(s)	
Other	
Power of Attorney (POA)	
Health-Care Directive	
Final Arrangement	
Ethical Will	
Will	
Trust	
Digital Estate Plan	
Pet Estate Plan	

ASSESSMENT

Based on your findings above, how are you doing financially at this point in time? Be specific.

_____

_____

_____

_____

_____

PLAN

What do you plan to do to improve your financial situation this year? Describe actions you will take and provide a timeline for completion with checkpoints and a deadline.

_____

_____

_____

_____

_____

Review Your Investment Policy Statement

Goal: The month of August is a great time to review your personal investment policy statement (IPS).

You can organize your investments by creating an investment policy statement, which serves as a road-map to managing your investment portfolio. An IPS provides an overview of your goals, objectives, asset allocation, risk tolerance, and investment policy. Your investment policy statement can help you transition from being an investment collector to an organized investor. Being organized will keep you focused on the big picture and prevent feelings of concern about short-term market changes.

☐ **Create Your Investment Policy Statement.** You can access a fillable Investment Policy Statement worksheet at tonysteuer.com.

    ☐ **Review Your Short-Term Financial Goals and Liquidity Needs.**

    ☐ **Review Your Long-Term Financial and Retirement Goals.**

        ☐ Complete the Get Ready! Retirement Tracker. *Get Ready!: A Step-by-Step Planner for Maintaining Your Financial First Aid Kit* provides a retirement-tracker worksheet to give you a general idea of where you are currently with your retirement planning and helps you plan out any changes. Access the Get Ready! Toolkit at tonysteuer.com.

☐ **Consider Your Investment Strategy and Objectives.** Is there a reason to make any changes to your IPS? Though I don't recommend chasing "hot" sectors or making any changes unless you have a good reason, this is an opportunity to revisit your overall strategy and objectives. Is there a new type of investment that makes sense for your portfolio? For example, when exchange-traded funds (ETFs) were introduced, they became a good alternative to mutual funds. Also, are there particular investments that should be removed from your portfolio?

☐ **Consider Your Risk Tolerance.** Is your risk tolerance shifting? As you get older, you may want to consider taking on less risk, especially if you're approaching retirement or in retirement. If you find your risk-tolerance level has changed, I recommend adjusting your asset allocation.

☐ **Review Your Asset Allocation Limits.** Asset allocation is about how much of your money is invested in a specific category of investment (stocks, bonds, cash, and other asset classes). Diversifying your assets will lower the volatility of your investment portfolio.

☐ **Think through Your Investment Selection Criteria.** Apply these criteria to every investment. Make sure your criteria are in line with your investment strategy.

☐ **Review Your Investment Balances.** Gathering your current information allows you to view your current asset totals and percentages of portfolio. As part of this, you'll want to include new investments and remove old investments.

☐ **Review Your Social Security Statements and Earnings History.** Order your statement at www.ssa.gov.

☐ **Consider Rebalancing.** You may want to consider rebalancing when allocations to your broad asset classes are outside your IPS's target range.

Review Your Investment Policy Statement

SUBJECTIVE

Summarize the goal for August. How do you feel about it?

_____

_____

_____

OBJECTIVE

Fill in the following table as you review your IPS:

Objectives (Goals)	
Investment Strategy	
Risk Tolerance	
Asset Allocation	
Investment Selection Criteria	
Current Investments	
Rebalancing Needed?	

Date when you requested your Social Security statement: _____

ASSESSMENT

Based on your findings above, how are you doing financially at this point in time? Be specific.

_____

_____

_____

_____

_____

_____

_____

PLAN

What do you plan to do to improve your financial situation this year? Describe actions you will take and provide a timeline for completion with checkpoints and a deadline.

_____

_____

_____

_____

_____

_____

_____

SEPTEMBER CHECKLIST

Review Your Insurance Policies

 Goal: Determine if your coverage still fits with your needs.

☐ **Confirm the Following Information for Each of Your Insurance Policies.** You can access fillable Insurance worksheets for help at tonysteuer.com.

　☐ **Do you need this type of coverage?** Major life events, like a family member's birth, death, change in marital status, job change, or retirement, may affect whether you still need coverage for specific types of insurance. Consider whether you may need to terminate certain policies.

　☐ **What is the coverage amount?** Based on your current situation, does it make sense to increase or reduce coverage for any particular policies?

　☐ **Is your information up-to-date?**

　☐ **Do you need to assess the financial strength of the company?** You can check the financial strength data of your insurance companies to help determine their ability to pay policy-holder claims by seeking their financial strength ratings with rating agencies.

　☐ **Have you looked into available discounts?**

　☐ **Are there any policy changes you need to review?**

　☐ **Does the premium still work for you?** Each insurance company uses its own method to calculate your premium. If you feel your premium is high, you sometimes have the option of reviewing alternative policies that may have lower premiums; when doing this, be sure to compare policies with similar policy parameters.

　☐ **Have you reviewed the deductible?** It's important to know that you have a deductible that provides the most value for you. You can visit tonysteuer.com/resources/find-optimal-insur-ance-deductible/ to access the Optimal Insurance Deductible Calculator on my site. I think everyone needs to ask themselves whether the money they save in insurance premiums jus-tifies taking on a higher risk, along with a higher deductible. The tool I offer on my website will calculate the additional risk that you are taking on and divide it by the annual savings to determine your break-even point.

Here are some specific insurance policy considerations:

☐ **Disability Insurance.** Review any exclusions, as they can sometimes be removed after a certain period. Consider also exercising any future purchase option or future increase options. And if you have coverage through your employer, you may want to consider an individual supplemental policy, as group coverage is oftentimes not sufficient.

☐ **Health Insurance.** Check that your preferred medical provider is still part of your health insurance company's network. It's also a good idea to review insurance company Explanation of Benefits (EOBs) for accuracy; these are not bills. As part of the Get Ready! Financial Calendar, you will review your individual and group health insurance in more detail in the month of October.

☐ **Homeowner's Insurance.** Look into increasing your coverage amounts if you have made home improve-ments or if replacement costs have risen in your area. As you think about making possible changes to your policy, consider also that earthquakes and floods are not typically covered under homeowner's insurance policies, but coverage may be obtained by adding an earthquake or flood endorsement to your homeowner's insurance policy or purchasing a stand-alone earthquake or flood policy.

☐ **Life Insurance.** If you have permanent life insurance, be sure to order an in-force illustration. For help on reviewing your life insurance, download the Annual Insurance Review guides from the Get Ready! Financial Preparedness Club resource center at tonysteuer.com.

SEPTEMBER SOAP NOTE
Review Your Insurance Policies

SUBJECTIVE

Summarize the goal for September. How do you feel about it?

_____

_____

_____

OBJECTIVE

Fill in the following table as you go through the process of reviewing your insurance policies:

INSURANCE TYPE	COVERAGE NEEDED?	FINANCIAL STRENGTH RATING	DISCOUNTS REVIEWED?
Auto			
Disability			
Health			
Homeowner's/Renter's			
Life			
Long-Term Care			
Annuity(ies)			
Other			

ASSESSMENT

Based on your findings above, how are you doing financially at this point in time? Be specific.

_____

_____

_____

_____

_____

PLAN

What do you plan to do to improve your financial situation this year? Describe actions you will take and provide a timeline for completion with checkpoints and a deadline.

_____

_____

_____

_____

_____

Review Open Enrollment for Group Employee Benefits, Health Insurance, and Medicare

 Goal: To review individual and group (employer) health insurance during open enrollment (including Medicare). Also review all other group employee benefits for open enrollment.

This is the month when open enrollment for employee (group) benefits and individual health insurance typically begins. Unless you have a qualifying event, this is the one time of year when you are able to make changes, so it's important to have an accurate view of your coverage and benefits.

Review your plan for changes to provider networks and to decide whether or not you need to make changes to your deductible and co-pays. The Health Care Costs and Health Insurance worksheets at tonysteuer.com can help you determine your true annual health-care costs. This will help you choose the optimal coverage. You can also use the Optimal Insurance Deductible Calculator on my website for some extra guidance on choosing your deductible.

- ☐ **Review Your Individual Health Insurance.** Individual health-care coverage open enrollment is usually from November 1 to December 15 for the Federal Health Care Insurance Exchange at healthcare.gov. Some states maintain their own health-care exchange and may have longer enrollment periods, so be sure to check with your state's exchange to confirm.

- ☐ **Review Your Medicare**. Medicare open enrollment usually begins October 15 and ends December 7. The Get Ready! Medicare worksheet at tonysteuer.com can help you review your coverage options. To learn more, visit www.medicare.gov.

- ☐ **Review Your Employee (Group) Benefits.** Open enrollment is your opportunity to add or remove dependents, make changes to your group insurance, plan contributions to flexible spending accounts, and cash out some of your time off and/or sick leave hours, if eligible. You'll want to also think about the following:

  - ☐ **Insurance.** Do you and your dependents have coverage outside of your employer? Compare the coverage provided and the premiums. In some cases, you may find you're better off enrolling on your spouse's plan rather than the one offered by your employer.

  - ☐ **Portability.** Most group insurance is not portable. Consider when an individual insurance policy is needed, based on your plans.

  - ☐ **Benefit credit.** Employers usually now provide a set credit, which is applied toward your cumulative employee benefits premiums and contributions rather than directly covering the premiums for each benefit.

  - ☐ **Disability insurance.** If needed, you have the opportunity during the open enrollment period to maximize the coverage available to you. You can also decide if you'd like to have your disability premiums paid on a post-tax basis so that your benefits are paid on an after-tax basis.

  - ☐ **Health insurance.** This is an excellent time for you to compare premiums, deductibles, co-pays, and total out-of-pocket limits. Be aware of changes in provider networks and pharmacy benefits managers.

  - ☐ **Life insurance.** Premiums for individual life insurance policies will usually be much lower for those in good health.

  - ☐ **Dental insurance.** Check if there is a waiting period before coverage starts and what the plan pays for, such as lab and material costs for crowns or bridges.

  - ☐ **Flexible Spending Account (FSA).** Plan out your contributions carefully. At open enrollment time, estimate what you will spend over the next calendar year. FSAs may allow you to carry over $500. Dependent Care Spending Accounts do not allow you to roll over any amount.

Be sure to review your benefit election confirmations to ensure that all of your elections and/or changes are correct. Corrections can usually only be made prior to the open enrollment deadline.

OCTOBER SOAP NOTE

Review Open Enrollment for Group Employee Benefits, Health Insurance, and Medicare

SUBJECTIVE

Summarize the goal for October. How do you feel about it?

_____

OBJECTIVE

Fill in the following information as you review your health insurance and benefits:

INSURANCE TYPE	COVERAGE NEEDED?	COVERAGE AMOUNT	PORTABLE	COMPARED
Disability				
Health				
Life				
Long-Term Care				
Other				

Individual health insurance open enrollment date: _____

Will you be making changes to your individual health insurance? _____

Do you have Medicare coverage? _____

Employer (group) open enrollment date: _____

Do you have dependents? How many? _____

What was your dependent care spending contribution amount last year? _____

What will your dependent care spending contribution amount be this year? _____

Have you reviewed your FSA funding? _____

Have you checked your benefit confirmation statement? _____

ASSESSMENT

Based on your findings above, how are you doing financially at this point in time? Be specific.

_____

_____

_____

_____

_____

PLAN

What do you plan to do to improve your financial situation this year? Describe actions you will take and provide a timeline for completion with checkpoints and a deadline.

_____

_____

_____

_____

_____

Order Credit Reports and Consumer Reports for Identity Monitoring

 Goal: Review information that is used to impact your financial life.

In today's environment of information freedom, it's important that you monitor and protect your identity.

☐ **Order Your Credit Reports.** Credit reports are compiled by credit reporting agencies, which are companies that collect information about where you live and work, how you pay your bills, and whether or not you have been sued, arrested, or have filed for bankruptcy. These companies sell your credit report to creditors, employers, insurers, and others, who then use these reports to make decisions about extending credit, jobs, and insurance policies to you. You are entitled to order a free copy of your credit report from each of the major credit reporting agencies—Equifax®, Experian®, and TransUnion®—every 12 months at www.annualcreditreport.com or by calling 877-322-8228. Please be aware that this website is the only one that is government-authorized to provide you with free copies of your credit report; many sites with similar URLs will either attempt to charge you or steal your personal information, so make sure to go to the correct website.

☐ **Review Your Credit Reports.**

　☐ **Use the Get Ready! Navigating Your Credit Report worksheet to help you understand and find your way around your credit reports.** You can access this worksheet at tonysteuer.com.

　☐ **Be sure to also review account status reporting, as statuses and dates can be incorrect, or debts can be listed twice.** This is important because you are likely the only person who can verify the accuracy of these reports. If you find something wrong with a credit report, you can file your dispute online at each credit reporting agency's website. To do this, explain what you think is wrong in the report and provide your reasons, along with any documentation to support your case.

☐ **Review Reports from Specialty Consumer Reporting Companies.** Many specialty consumer-reporting companies collect and share information about your employment history, transaction history with businesses, or repayment histories for specific products or services. You should review your consumer reports because you are likely the only person who can verify the accuracy of the information they contain. I recommend requesting reports from the following entities:

　☐ **LexisNexis.** This consumer report includes items such as real estate transactions and ownership data; lien, judgment, and bankruptcy records; professional license information; and historical addresses on file. You can request your report at personalreports.lexisnexis.com.

　☐ **C.L.U.E. Report.** Also from LexisNexis, this report includes information on insurance claims histories for auto insurance and homeowner's insurance. You can request your report at personalreports.lexisnexis.com/fact_act_disclosure.jsp.

　☐ **Medical Information Bureau (MIB).** You will have an MIB file if you have applied for individual life insurance, disability insurance, or health insurance within the last seven years. MIB doesn't have actual reports or medical records on file but its records do contain coded information that identifies any medical conditions or medical tests reported by other MIB members regarding a particular applicant. You can request your report at www.mib.com/request_your_record.html.

　☐ **The Work Number.** This report compiles employment and income information. It is used by lenders, property managers, pre-employment screeners, social service agencies, and others who need to verify someone's employment status and sometimes his or her income as well. You can request your report at www.theworknumber.com.

NOVEMBER SOAP NOTE

Order Credit Reports and Consumer Reports for Identity Monitoring

SUBJECTIVE

Summarize the goal for November. How do you feel about it?

_____

_____

_____

OBJECTIVE

Fill in the following table as you order and review your credit and consumer reports:

REPORT	DATE ORDERED	DATE RECEIVED	DISPUTES
Equifax®			
Experian®			
TransUnion®			
LexisNexis			
C.L.U.E. Report			
Medical Information Bureau			
The Work Number			
Other			

ASSESSMENT

Based on your findings above, how are you doing financially at this point in time? Be specific.

_____

_____

_____

_____

_____

_____

_____

PLAN

What do you plan to do to improve your financial situation this year? Describe actions you will take and provide a timeline for completion with checkpoints and a deadline.

_____

_____

_____

_____

_____

_____

_____

Wrap Up Loose Ends

 Goal: Complete your financial first aid kit maintenance before the end of the year.

☐ **Wrap up Loose Ends.** Circle back to previous goals on the Get Ready! Financial Calendar that still need your attention.

☐ **To End Your Year Well, Consider These Other Action Items in December:**

    ☐ **Make a holiday budget.** List out your gift recipients and how much you would like to spend on each of them.

    ☐ **Be careful about piling up credit card charges.** Be sure you can pay off your December balance with your next statement, so you can avoid high interest charges.

    ☐ **Decide whether you will use any gift cards you have.** If you are not going to use them, consider whether you can re-gift them, or consider selling them.

    ☐ **Keep your individual health-care enrollment deadline in mind.** The deadline for the Federal Health Insurance Exchange is usually December 15. States with their own exchanges may have longer open enrollment periods, so check your state website as well.

    ☐ **Review your spending account balances, so you can file your claims.** Dependent Care Spending Accounts (DCSAs) and many Flexible Spending Accounts (FSAs) have a "use it or lose it" policy. If you know you're going to have money left over, here are a few applicable expenses for FSAs you might like to consider (visit www.irs.gov and search for flexible spending accounts to see a complete and current list):

        ☐ Vision (new glasses or contacts)

        ☐ Chiropractic care

        ☐ Acupuncture

        ☐ Prescription medications

        ☐ Mental health treatment (therapy)

    ☐ **Make charitable donations.** This is the month to make any year-end donations to support your favorite nonprofits and causes. Be sure to check to see if your donation is tax deductible and if so, remember to claim your tax deduction in the coming year.

    ☐ **Complete any gifts to people or trusts.** Doing this allows you to take advantage of the annual gift tax exclusion. The annual gift tax exclusion limits increase each year.

    ☐ **Review your IRA and 401(k) contributions and distributions.** If you had to take a first required minimum distribution (RMD) by April 1, you must take your second RMD by December 31.

    ☐ **Conduct an Unclaimed Property Search.** Have you ever wondered what it would be like to receive money that you weren't expecting? There are many free and easy ways to search to see if you have unclaimed money. All of these services can be accessed directly and at no cost. There is hardly ever a good reason to pay a service to locate money for you. You can access an Unclaimed Property Search Checklist at tonysteuer.com.

DECEMBER SOAP NOTE

Wrap Up Loose Ends

SUBJECTIVE

Summarize the goal for December. How do you feel about it?

_____

_____

_____

OBJECTIVE

Fill in the following table as you go through the process of ending the year financially well:

Holiday Budget?	
Health Insurance Enrollment Completed?	
Dependent Care Spending Accounts (DCSAs) and Flexible Spending Accounts (FSAs) Reimbursements Made?	
Charitable Donations Made?	
Gifts Completed?	
IRA and 401(k) Contributions and Distributions Reviewed and Action Taken?	
Unclaimed Property Search Done?	

ASSESSMENT

Based on your findings above, how are you doing financially at this point in time? Be specific.

_____

_____

_____

_____

_____

_____

_____

_____

PLAN

What do you plan to do to improve your financial situation this year? Describe actions you will take and provide a timeline for completion with checkpoints and a deadline.

_____

_____

_____

_____

_____

_____

_____

_____

Final Thoughts

THANK YOU FOR TAKING THE TIME TO COMPLETE *The Get Ready! Monthly Personal Finance Guidebook.* I hope you are feeling organized and ready for the financial situations in your life.

If you loved the guidebook or *Get Ready!: A Step-by-Step Planner for Maintaining Your Financial First Aid Kit* and have a minute to spare, I would really appreciate a short review on your favorite book or e-commerce site. You're the reason why I continue to write about financial preparedness and advocate for integrity in financial services.

If you think this guidebook or planner might help a family member or friend with their own financial preparedness, feel free to invite them to access the Get Ready! Toolkit at tonysteuer.com. They can receive useful information and monthly email tips to show them how they might complete a financial first aid kit of their own.

To stay up-to-date on the latest in financial preparedness and access the Get Ready! Toolkit, visit tonysteuer.com to subscribe to my newsletter and join the Get Ready! community.

About the Author

TONY STEUER is on a mission to help people be prepared for any financial emergency. He shows consumers how to create their own financial first aid kit and is the founder of the Get Ready! Initiative, which includes the Get Ready! Financial Standards, Get Ready! Organization System, Get Ready! Principles, Get Ready! Toolkit, Get Ready! Newsletter, Get Ready! Podcast, and the Get Ready! Financial Literacy Resource Directory. Tony also provides best practices for financial advisors and insurance agents to follow to ensure that their clients are fully prepared for financial emergencies.

He has led the way in establishing a path for financial preparedness through his award winning books:

Insurance Made Easy
Questions and Answers on Life Insurance: The Life Insurance Toolbook
The Questions and Answers on Life Insurance Workbook
The Questions and Answers on Disability Insurance Workbook
The Questions and Answers on Insurance Planner
Get Ready!: A Step-by-Step Planner for Maintaining Your Financial First Aid Kit

Tony regularly consults with insuretechs, financial planners, insurance agencies, attorneys, insurance companies, and other financial service companies on insurance marketing and product best practices and on strategies to help consumers Get Ready! through financial preparedness and the Get Ready! Initiative. Tony is a past member of the California Department of Insurance Curriculum Board and the National Financial Educators Council (NFEC) Curriculum Advisory Board.

He is regularly featured in the media. Tony has appeared in interviews for the *New York Times*, the *Washington Post*, *U.S. News & World Report*, *CNBC*, *Fast Company*, Slate.com, BottomLine Personal, Bankrate.com, Insure.com, InsuranceQuotes.com, Mint.com, and BenefitsPro.com. He has appeared as a guest on the ABC7 KGO's *Seven On Your Side*, Gritdaily, Cheddar TV, *Wall Street Journal Morning Radio Show, Prudent Money Show, Your Financial Editor, Insider Secrets, Suzy G. in the Morning Show, Financial Finesse,* GrowingMoney.com, Nolo.com, TheNest.com, LovetoKnow.com, and LifeInsuranceSelling.com. Tony also served as a technical editor for *The Retirement Bible* and *The Investing Bible*.

Made in the USA
Monee, IL
11 March 2021